Mudge, Gill and Steve

ST.MARY'S UNIVERSITY COLLEGE LIBRARY

A COLLEGE OF THE QUEENS UNIVERSITY OF BELFAST

Tel: 028 90327678   Web Site: www.stmarys-belfast.ac.uk   email: library@stmarys-belfast.ac.uk

'I am impressed by this book because it covers so many important facets of bereavement with such a lightness of touch and even humour, and forms a moving testimony to the bitter-sweet nature of existence. The theology beneath the story is clear, Bible-based and is sensibly combined with a realistic view of life.

I would commend the book as a useful tool for all clergy, schools, parents and carers dealing with children who have had experience of bereavement thrust upon them at such a tender age. This sensitive and gentle book will ease any understandable reticence or even dread they may have in approaching such situations.'

David Hope, Archbishop of York

'Jim Dainty writes out of real experience in the context of ordinary life. No two children have identical needs and no book can provide all the answers, but I believe that Mudge, Gill and Steve *will go a long way towards comforting many children who are experiencing the loneliness of bereavement.'*

Sister Frances Dominica, Helen House Children's Hospice

Mudge, Gill and Steve

A children's guide to bereavement

JAMES DAINTY

Illustrations by
CHRISTINE BERRINGTON

National Society/Church House Publishing
Church House, Great Smith Street, London SW1P 3NZ

Church House Publishing
Church House
Great Smith Street
London SW1P 3NZ

ISBN 0 7151 4887 7

Published 1997 by The National Society and Church House
Publishing

Cover design by Christine Berrington
Printed in England by The Cromwell Press Ltd, Melksham, Wiltshire.

Dedicated to the children
of the Leeds hospitals

Introduction

G'day kids,

I just loved this story about Mudge – what a character!
I think you'll enjoy reading it too.

There is also something special about this story,
because it helps us to find answers to some hard
questions about death.

Death is not easy to talk about or to explain. Most
people seem to be afraid to talk about death at all,
and that's why some of the things that grown ups
say can be confusing.

What Mudge discovers in the story will be a help
for you too – it was for Gill and Steve.

lots of love,
Rolf Harris

(P.S. If you're reading this with a grown up, tell
them there is a letter for them, from Gill and Steve,
at the end of the book.)

1
Mudge finds a new home

Gill believed that names were important. So when a very big black dog came to live with them, she asked, "What's its name?"

Mum said, "She is called 'Smudge' because of the smudge of white on her nose."

"I think she looks like a 'Mudgey Moo Cow'!" laughed Steve.

Mum explained, "Smudge is a Great Dane and one of the biggest sorts of dog. Because she's so big, there may be times when we'll think we've invited a small cow to come and live with us! But she's so gentle and loving, I think we're going to enjoy having her."

"Well," said Gill thoughtfully, "I think you're beautiful and we'll call you 'Mudge', because it's easy to say and it sounds like your old name."

So that day, Mudge got a new home, a new family and a new name. She also got a bright red collar, with a disc engraved with her new name.

The children thought it was a huge adventure as they followed the big dog exploring her new house. There were so many new smells and surprises. Mudge had never seen stairs before and so Steve helped her climb them one by one, so she could visit their bedrooms. However when it came to going back down, Mudge found stairs looked very dangerous. She sat on the top step and refused to budge.

The children tried pushing, and pulling and shouting. But she was so frightened that she couldn't move.

In the end Steve had to fetch Dad, and he had to pick up Mudge in his arms and carry her down again. That wasn't easy, but she was very gentle and happy to be carried.

Gill and Steve knew what fear felt like. There had been times when they had that strange feeling in their tummies, and their throats felt all dry and it was difficult to swallow. It reminded them of how they had felt when they had gone through the hole in their garden wall.

2

The hole in the wall

It was while playing football that they found the hole. They had lost the ball in between the hedges. Then there it was – the ball was just to the side of some bricks that had fallen and left a hole in the wall.

It was very dark behind the hedges. When they looked through the hole they could see everything was overgrown on the other side. Gill decided that they should have a look, and climbed into the next-door garden.

They knew no one lived there. They had seen the house from the street and it looked cold and empty. But now as they looked across the garden of thistles and overgrown plants and bushes, it was rather frightening. Some windows were broken and some-where in the house, as the wind blew, it was making a door open and then shut with a "bang"!

They did not know why, but they didn't feel safe, and soon they were back through the hole and in their own garden.

Their new dog Mudge particularly liked their garden. There was space to run and play all kinds of games, and soon she discovered the hole in the wall too. When Dad was there it felt safe for them all to play hide and seek. Steve and Gill would climb through the hole in the wall and hide in the extra tall grass. Then Dad would send Mudge through to find them. They didn't feel frightened then – it was different. They felt excited because they knew at any moment a big black nose would push through the grass, and they'd be greeted with a lick and happy barking.

3

Mudge welcomes the new neighbours

Mudge didn't give up easily, and before too long she had learned to climb up and down the stairs on her own.

Steve ran to tell Mum. "Mum, guess what, Mudge can get down stairs on her own, come and see."

Mum watched Mudge run up the stairs, and then climb down rather slowly. Then she said, "I've got some news for you. We've got some new neighbours. They're going to live in the empty house. They've been very busy getting the house ready, and this morning they've moved in with all their furniture."

"When can we meet them?" said Gill.

"I've invited them to come and have some tea with us, when they've finished unpacking all their things," Mum explained.

The children rushed to open the door when the doorbell rang. As soon as the door opened Mudge stood on her back legs and put her paws on Mr Wint's shoulders. He got quite a surprise as she gave him a lick on his cheek.

"Hello, my name's Simon, and this is my wife Miriam," said Mr Wint. "You must be Mudge! You're the friendliest dog I've ever met."

"Hello," said Miriam to Gill and Steve. "You can call us 'Uncle Simon and Auntie Miriam' if you want to, because we hope to become good friends."

Gill and Steve said, "Hello."

They all liked Uncle Simon and Auntie Miriam. They were great fun, and they did become good friends. When Steve was asked who he wanted to come to his fifth birthday party, the first people he wanted to invite were Auntie Miriam and Uncle Simon!

That Christmas was special too. Grandma came to stay, although this time she was on her own. There were many presents. The Wints invited them all to a special party, and Mudge was invited too.

It was good being together in the house next door. They had lots of food and games to play, and Uncle Simon told amazing stories. Mudge snuggled up close as they listened. It was all so different from the time when they went through the hole in the wall, and saw the house so dark and empty. Now it was warm and a place where their friends lived.

4
Mudge welcomes
a new baby

Mum and Miriam had become special friends. They shared recipes, knitting patterns and news. One day, Gill and Steve heard them say that a new baby was coming to stay. Auntie Miriam seemed to laugh and smile even more than usual.

"I think Auntie Miriam must be eating too many sweets," said Steve, "she's starting to get fat."

Mum explained, "It's not too many sweets. She's going to have a baby. The baby is growing inside her and when it's big enough it will be born."

"Is it nearly ready yet?" asked Gill.

It did seem such a long time to wait. But the time came when Mum said, "Today is a birthday! Auntie Miriam went into hospital this morning and her baby has been born there."

"I thought hospitals were for people who were ill," said Steve.

"They are", said Mum, "but sometimes things can go wrong when a baby is born. That's why it's good to be in a place where doctors and nurses are ready to help."

"What's the baby's name?" asked Gill.

"He's a little boy called Joe," said Mum.

"Was I born in hospital?" Steve wanted to know.

"Yes," said Mum.

"And me too?" asked Gill.

"Yes, and you too," replied Mum.

"I want to see Joe," said Gill.

"He'll be coming home in two days," said Mum.

When Joe arrived at his home, Gill, Steve, Mudge, Mum and Dad went to say "welcome". Everyone was so happy. Mudge gave Joe a lick on his toes, and Joe must have liked that because he gave a big smile.

Steve and Gill wondered what Uncle Simon meant when he said that Joe was a gift. How could Joe be a present?

They understood a little more when they went to church together. Reverend Mr Smith held a special service for Joe. He said Joe was a gift from God. It was God who made it possible for the Wints to have a new baby.

In the prayers they said "thank you" to God for loving their baby. They told God that the name they had chosen for him was "Joseph Christopher", although they usually called him "Joe".

5

An anxious night

It was a cold and wet day. When Steve and Gill arrived home from school, they were told to go and play quietly. Dad and Uncle Simon were talking very seriously. Mudge was sitting with them listening, and it looked very private and important.

At tea-time Dad told them that Joe had been taken into hospital. "He has a problem with his heart, and the doctors think he may need a big operation. Things are not quite right."

"Poor little chap," said Mum, "he's not quite a year old, and so very small."

Steve and Gill felt very sad, but they didn't know what to say, so they just ate their tea and listened. There was a lot of anxious talk between Mum and Dad. Gill said a prayer quietly, so no one could hear, and asked Jesus to help the doctors to make Joe well again.

Later, just as Dad was saying "good night" to them as they were getting ready to go to sleep, there was a knock at the door. Mum called Dad to come. Gill and Steve got out of their beds and looked down the stairs into the kitchen. Uncle Simon was standing quietly with his head held back a little. His hands were clenched tightly. Tears were rolling down his face. Auntie Miriam was wrapped up in Mum's arms. She was shaking and sobbing, "I've lost my Joe, I've lost my Joe."

Steve whispered to Gill, "I'm sure Mudge could find Joe. I wonder where they've lost him? I think it would be at the hospital – it's a very big place." Gill told him to "Shut up", and they went silently back to bed. But it wasn't easy to sleep with so many thoughts going round in their heads.

6

A sad morning

Next morning at breakfast, Mum and Dad looked tired. They hadn't slept very well. Steve wondered if it might be all right to ask if Joe was still lost. But before he could, Dad said he'd something to tell them. There were tears in his eyes when he told them that Joe had died.

"I thought he was lost," said Steve. "We heard you say last night that he was lost."

"That's what people say," explained Dad. "When you've something very precious and then you don't have it anymore – that is a great loss. There was nothing more precious to Uncle Simon and Auntie Miriam, than little Joe. And now they have him no longer it's a great loss."

Gill felt very strange inside when she thought that she would never see Joe again. She loved him and would miss him. She remembered being allowed to hold him when he was very small, and playing together when he was bigger and had learned to crawl.

Steve was full of questions. "Why did he die? Was it because he was ill?"

"Yes," said Mum, "but it wasn't like when you've been ill. There was something wrong with his heart. It is a very special part of you – you can sometimes feel it working when you put your hand on your chest."

"Why didn't the doctors make it right?" asked Gill.

Mum began to cry, and said very gently, "They can do many clever things, but Joe was too poorly. Sadly, he died."

"Why are you crying?" asked Steve.

"Because we are so sad. We miss Joe and we loved him so much. We are sad for Simon and Miriam because they loved Joe and they had plans and hopes for him. Now none of their dreams for Joe can happen, because a precious part of their family is missing," Mum said, through her tears.

7

A walk
in the woods

Gill didn't feel comfortable with Mum crying. She gave Mum a hug and hoped the tears would stop. Then she remembered that it was Saturday. "We don't have to go to school today," she said, "and Dad doesn't have to go to work. Can we take Mudge for a long walk in the woods?"

"Yes, that's what I want," said Steve, who wished to think about something different. The washing-up was done. Gill got the lead for Mudge and Steve got a ball. They were soon ready to go.

In the woods they ran and chased. Mudge went in front as if to make sure all was safe. Gill got hold of Dad's hand, and walked along with him. When she'd sorted out what she wanted to say, she asked, "Why was Joe born with a heart that wasn't right?"

"Do you remember when you asked Mum if you could make a Christmas cake?" asked Dad.

"Yes," she said, "but what's that got to do with Joe?"

"I was thinking of what happened to you. You got all the things together that you needed, you asked Mum to tell you what to do, and then she let you make it all on your own."

"I remember," said Gill, "it was a bit burnt. It tasted so bad we could hardly eat it! I gave some to Mudge and she chewed it and then left it on the side of her bowl."

"How did you feel?" asked Dad.

"I was sad and angry, because I wanted it to be good and I tried ever so hard. It was so unfair. Mum wasn't cross, because she was sad as well. She wanted it to turn out right too," remembered Gill.

Dad went on to say, "Well, it's a very complicated thing making a Christmas cake. There is so much that can go wrong. It's very special when Mum lets you try on your very own. But it's much more difficult to make a whole new person, and because we are so complicated, sometimes things go wrong."

"Like with Joe?" interrupted Gill.

"Yes, like with Joe. I don't think God made Joe with a heart that was wrong. I think it was something that happened, and when it did, I think God was sad too."

Gill was quiet for a while. Then she asked, "Why did God let Joe die? In my prayer I asked Jesus to help the doctors, to make him better."

Dad thought for a minute or two and then said, "There are some questions we can't answer. The Bible does say that death is a bad thing because it takes our friends away from us. But to die is safe. God doesn't take away our friends. It's death that does that. Jesus comes to people like Joe after they have died. Jesus gives them new life so they can live with him in heaven. Usually people don't die until they're old. When someone dies who is young, or still a child, it seems very unfair."

Just then Mudge stood right in front of them in the path, and barked. When she did this it meant she was ready to turn round and go home. Mum or Dad usually had a biscuit for Mudge in their pockets. Mudge then stood in the way and barked to tell them that she was ready for the "turn round biscuit".

"Is it time to go back?" shouted Steve, who was climbing a tree.

"Mudge says it is," said Mum, as she gave the dog her biscuit.

"You're a funny old dog," said Gill, and then they all set off for home with Mudge leading the way.

8
Mudge makes a splash

Later, when they were back home, Mum commented, "You were quiet for a long time up that tree, Steve."

"That was because I was thinking," he said. "I was thinking about what it was like to be dead. Does it hurt?"

"No, it doesn't hurt. People usually look very peaceful when they die. They can look just as if they're asleep. But they're not, going to sleep is quite different. We go to sleep when we're tired and wake up feeling fit and fresh."

"Dying is a bit like when you went through the hole in the wall. It didn't hurt, but it was very strange, and so you were anxious. But you said you weren't afraid when Mudge was there with you. The Bible says that when a person dies, God will be there to meet them and take away any fear."

Mudge followed them as they made their way upstairs to the bathroom. Steve started to take his clothes off for his bath. He still looked deep in thought, so Mum continued . . .

"You told me about the empty house next door, and how it was cold and broken. The people who lived there had moved on somewhere else. Our bodies are like that. When we die, we move on and we don't need them anymore. Jesus has promised us new bodies that will never wear out or get sick."

Mum saw another question coming, and said, "Before you ask, the answer is 'No'. No one can come along and repair the body of someone who has died! I know Simon Wint repaired the empty house and made it a new home. But you're not a house – you're a person."

"And a person with very dirty hands and face after tree climbing! I think you'd better put your body in the bath."

They had a laugh and a cuddle together as they waited for the bath to fill. Suddenly, just as Mum was looking in the cupboard for some new soap, there was a loud "splash" and water flew through the air. There sitting in the bath was Mudge, with a very confused look on her face. She had jumped into the water!

Steve laughed and laughed at the funny dog.

"What we need here is a plan," said Mum. "Steve, you put your dressing gown on and keep warm. There is no room for you in a bath full of this big dog. Mudge, you're going to find out what we use the bath for . . . I shall wash and shampoo you till you smell as sweet as a bunch of flowers! Steve, you can help me. Then we will fill the bath with clean water again, and wash you afterwards."

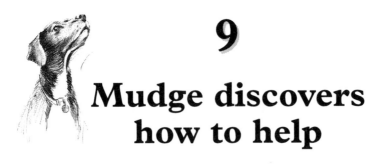

9
Mudge discovers how to help

"Let's invite Simon and Miriam round for a meal tomorrow," said dad.

After church, Simon and Miriam arrived. Miriam wanted to help Mum get the food ready. Simon sat quietly and began to talk to Mudge, who had climbed up beside him on the sofa. She was lying with her head on his knee – as if she was listening.

"You know Mudge, you've been a real friend and a help to me in all this sad time," he said.

Steve tried to think of what Mudge had done to help. He couldn't think of anything. Eventually he asked, "How has Mudge helped?"

Simon explained that when he had gone to the local shop there were some people there who knew that Joe had died. When they saw him and Miriam in the shop, they turned and walked away. It had been like that at church that morning. Lots of people had seen them, and then turned away, as if they hadn't seen them. "They do this because they don't know what to say, and they are afraid that they may say something wrong."

"That's true," thought Steve, "I've not really said anything to Uncle Simon or Auntie Miriam since Joe died."

"But," continued Uncle Simon, "we don't need special words. We just need someone to be there with us. That is why Mudge is such a help. She snuggles up as if to say 'I love you, I am sorry you are sad, can I just be with you?'"

Steve listened as Mr Wint and Dad talked about a special service Reverend Mr Smith was going to have for Joe. It was called a funeral. There were going to be prayers asking God to take care of Joe until the day when we all meet again, in heaven. Reverend Mr Smith told Mr Wint that in that part of the service they would be saying "Goodbye" to Joe.

Uncle Simon began to laugh. "Do you remember that funny song which always made Joe laugh when I sang it? Well, we've got a recording of it and we're going to play it at the service. So that will bring back lots of happy memories of Joe."

Mum and Miriam came in with the food. Dad told Mudge to get down off the sofa. Great Danes are such big dogs that if they are allowed to get on to furniture they damage it. Mudge pretended to be asleep, until Dad sounded cross, then she got down very slowly and wandered off to see if there was any food in her bowl.

When Gill and Mum were able to be together, on their own, Gill said, "I wonder why Uncle Simon laughed when he was talking about the service for Joe? Isn't he supposed to be sad?"

"I was just thinking about that myself," said Mum. "I was thinking how strange it is that we can have more than one feeling at the same time. We can be sad, and also feel happiness as we remember Joe. We can also feel safe and know that all will be well. Jesus said that God our Father will never let a little one like Joe be left out of his great plans for us in heaven. God loves Joe even more than we do."

"I don't know what to feel," said Gill. "Sometimes I feel very sad and I want to cry. At other times I think it must be lovely for Joe to be in heaven, and so I don't need to feel sorry for him. But I still miss him, because he was fun."

"Most people find they can't choose how they feel," Mum explained. "Very often when we have had a sadness, our feelings get all jumbled up."

10

Double dinner for Mudge

It was lunch-time on Saturday, when the door burst open and Mudge came charging through the house with Gill and Steve close behind. They had been up to the park and when they returned they just opened the door a little and Mudge pushed her way in. It was past her dinner-time and she needed to check her bowl to see if her food had arrived. She had a very large bowl and it was empty. So Dad brought a big tin of meat from the cupboard and opened it. Soon Mudge was chomping her way through her dinner, wagging her tail in a very happy fashion.

It was a moment or two before Steve and Gill noticed that Uncle Simon and Auntie Miriam had arrived. Mum had opened the door to them, while Dad was getting dinner for Mudge.

Suddenly Mum demanded in a very loud voice, "What's that dog doing?"

"She's having her dinner!" explained Steve and Gill, wondering why Mum should ask and sound cross.

"But I fed her a whole tin of meat for her dinner before you took her out to the park!" said Mum.

They all laughed and Mudge continued to eat, looking very happy, with her tail still wagging.

"She probably thinks it's her birthday!" Dad exclaimed.

As he said this, Auntie Miriam stopped laughing and quietly started to cry. Uncle Simon put his arm round her. He explained that they were sad because if Joe had still been alive, that day would have been his first birthday.

Mum made some tea and they were able to sit quietly together. Very gently, Dad asked, "When are the hardest times for you, when you miss Joe most?"

Auntie Miriam said, "Today would have been a very special day, we would have had a party. I think the special days will be when we will miss Joe most. Days like Christmas, and birthdays. But any day can bring back our sad feelings. When we see other children growing up and being together with their parents, we miss Joe a lot."

11

Mudge appears in pictures

Gill and Steve realised that some days they never thought about Joe at all. They wondered if that would that mean they might forget him. How could they make sure they didn't forget him?

"Do you think we will always remember Joe?" asked Gill.

"I am sure we will," replied Mum. "All the happy memories of him come back every time I look at his picture."

She went to the shelf and took down the photograph album. When she reached the page with Joe's photo, they all smiled. It was a picture of Joe in the garden. He had a great big grin on his face and was waving his hands in the air.

Steve decided that photos were brilliant. He had used Mum's camera sometimes and knew how it worked. He thought that all the important people in his life must have their photo taken as soon as possible. Quietly, and without asking, he collected Mum's camera and went off into the garden with Mudge.

It was not very long before he and Mudge returned. He carefully put the camera down on a shelf, next to a picture of Grandpa, and asked, "Is it a long time since Grandpa went to be with Jesus?"

Mum and Dad looked at each other, and then Dad said, "Steve, it was the summer before the last one, just before the school holidays. Grandpa was getting quite old and then he was ill for a short time, and didn't get better. We were glad for him that he died, because he had become so tired and unwell. Now he has no more pain and is safe with Jesus. But it's sad for us, because we loved him so much and miss him."

"We did tell you about Grandpa. Don't you remember that time when we were all so sad? It was just after you'd started school, Steve, and you were away because you had an upset tummy."

Mum reminded them about how Gill had gone to school and Dad had looked after Steve, while she had gone on the train to the town where Grandpa's funeral took place.

"I remember," said Gill.

"We didn't talk much about Grandpa dying," said Dad. "We did tell you, but we didn't want you to be too upset. So just Mum and I made plans about the best thing to do."

"We did wonder about all of us going to the funeral. But it was such a long way and Steve was poorly, so only I went," added Mum.

"What happened when you got there?" asked Steve.

"We had a service and lots of Grandpa's friends came. We remembered all the good things about him, and said 'thank you' to God for giving us such a good friend. We said 'thank you' to God for what Jesus has done for us to bring us new life. Then we had a prayer when we asked God to take care of Grandma and all of us, and to help us by sharing with us in our sadness."

"Did you do any singing?" wondered Gill.

"Yes, we sang two of Grandpa's favourite hymns," said Mum.

"Then what happened?" asked Steve.

Mum told them, "The body that Grandpa didn't need anymore, which he had left behind when he died, had been placed in a wooden box called a coffin. After the service, the coffin was placed in a special hole in the ground called a grave. Then it was covered over with soil and some flowers were left on the top. The place where the graves are is called a cemetery."

They were quiet for a short time. Then Gill said, "I haven't forgotten Grandpa. He loved us a lot and we loved him."

"I remember him too," added Steve. "But I think it is terrific that I know someone in heaven! My own Grandpa is in heaven with Jesus. And now I'm going to watch my TV programme."

"Me too," said Gill as she went to join Steve, in the room where the TV was.

After they'd gone, Mum went over to look at the photo of Grandpa. Next to it she found her camera was out, and not in the place where she kept it. As she was putting it away she noticed that the button was stuck. It seemed odd, because she had only recently put a new film in it. So she asked Dad to take it to the photographers and have it checked.

Two days later, when Dad collected the camera, Mum asked, "Was it broken?"

"No, it was not broken," he replied, "and here are some pictures to prove it." Then he placed them on the table. They were all of Mudge. Sitting, stand-ing, lying, rolling, running, jumping . . . 36 pictures of one dog.

"I took them," said Steve. "I wanted to always be able to remember Mudge, and think about her every day."

When Mudge heard them talking about her she climbed up to look at the pictures.

"You should have asked first, before using the camera . . . and you don't need a photo when a dog as big as this lives in our house!" said Dad.

Gill didn't seem interested in seeing the photos. Mum noticed how quiet she was, and said, "You look as if you've got a problem you can't solve."

"My friend Louise told me at school today, that when you are dead they don't put you in a hole in the ground," Gill blurted out, " . . . they burn you. She knows because that is what they did to her auntie. I told Louise what you said about Grandpa and the service you went to, but she said it isn't true."

Mum could see the anxious feelings in Gill. She put her arm around her, gave her a hug, and suggested they sit down together.

They sat quietly for a time and then Mum said, "Gill, what I told you was absolutely true. But," she continued, "Louise was right in some ways too. Did she go to her auntie's funeral?"

"No," said Gill, "but her big brother did and he told her."

"It sounds as if what he told her was rather frightening. Would you like me to tell you about it? It shouldn't make you afraid and it might help?"

"I'm not sure, but I think I want to know," said Gill.

Mum reminded Gill of what happens when someone dies. "You know how I told you about Grandpa, and how when a person dies they leave behind a body they don't need anymore?"

"Yes," said Gill.

"Well that body can't feel anything. It can't feel any hurts. It can't be repaired – no one lives there anymore. So what do you think can be done with such a body?" asked Mum.

"I suppose it could be left alone, or put in a hole in the ground like you said happened to Grandpa," answered Gill.

"We couldn't just leave a body," explained Mum, "because it would make people very unhappy, and seem as if we didn't care. But you are right, we can place a body in the ground. And there is another way, which is what Louise's brother told her about. This other way is given a strange name – it is called 'cremation'."

Mum continued, "When someone dies, people have a service for their friend who has died. The place looks like a church, but there's another special room. When the service ends and the people have gone, the body is taken into that other room and put in what looks like a big oven. Only the people who work there see this happen. Louise's brother wouldn't have seen this, and certainly wouldn't have seen any fire or flames.

"The heat in the oven makes the body change to what is called 'ashes'. These are then placed in a smaller box, rather like a coffin, and often they're then placed in a hole in the ground, with some special stone to mark the place. On the stone is written the name of the person who died. This helps us to remember them."

Gill was very quiet. It was a lot to think about. She felt rather grown up to be told about what happened. She also thought it better not to tell Steve, because it was a bit hard to understand. She wondered if she should tell Louise.

"Are you sure it doesn't hurt, and that it couldn't happen to someone who was still alive?" she asked.

Mum reassured her, "That's not possible. Two doctors have to check to see that a person is really dead – that they have left their body behind. And it certainly doesn't hurt at all. You know how we cut your toe nails and your hair and they don't hurt. Yet if you cut your knee, it really does hurt."

Gill nodded.

"In the body of a person who has died there is no part that can feel anything at all. Everything has come to an end."

"But remember people are not put in a grave or cremated – only bodies that people don't need anymore. It doesn't hurt."

"The people who work at such places have very special feelings of respect and do their work very carefully."

"Feelings like that are called 'solemn' feelings because something very serious is happening. I think we've got feelings like that right now, because we've been talking about such serious things. It's time we thought of something else and had a change of feelings! Tell me, what did you leave on the table when you came home?"

Gill remembered. "Oh that . . . come and see . . . it's something we made at school. See if you can guess what it's for," she said.

She got up and took her mother by the hand, and together they went to investigate.

12

Where do Great Danes sleep?

Having a big dog in the house was something they'd all become used to. It meant that sometimes they'd have to step over her, if she was asleep in a doorway. Sometimes they had to wait to go up stairs, if Mudge was coming down, because there wouldn't be room to pass.

They also knew that they had to keep a close watch on any food that was on the table, because Mudge was tall enough to see it and reach over and eat it.

Sometimes life got more difficult. If Mudge went to sleep in front of their drawers or clothes' cupboard, Mum or Dad would have to come and wake her up and move her before Gill and Steve could get to their things.

Steve made a joke about living with Mudge. It happened one night after supper, when it was time to go to bed and they were about to go upstairs. They found their way was blocked. Mudge was sleeping with her feet on the floor, her body on the second step and her head resting on the third step. She was gently snoring and Dad had to come to move her.

It was then Steve thought of his joke.

"Where do Great Danes sleep?" he asked.

They looked at each other. They all thought it must be a trick question, but no one knew the answer.

"Anywhere they want to!" laughed Steve.

Then they all laughed, because it was true. Mudge felt so safe with them that when she was tired, she would just lie down and go to sleep anywhere.

"She often sleeps next to my bed, and stays there all night," said Gill. "I like that, because I love her, and I think she likes to be with me because she loves me too."

"I expect she'd really like to sleep next to my bed sometimes," said Steve, "but there isn't much room with all my toys, and my train set."

They talked for a short time and then said their prayers. They thanked Jesus for loving them, and for all the friends who loved them. They asked Jesus to take care of Grandma, and Uncle Simon and Auntie Miriam and Mum and Dad, and Joe and Grandpa.

"And thank you for our lovely dog, Mudge. Amen," ended Steve.

He then opened his eyes and discovered she wasn't there. He thought she must have gone back downstairs. So he went to his bed, but found he couldn't get in. Mudge was stretched out, on his bed, asleep with her head on his pillow!

Dad had followed them upstairs, and just before he woke Mudge and got her to move off the bed, he quietly asked, "Where do Great Danes sleep?"

"Anywhere they want to!" shouted Steve.

13

A letter
to grown ups

Dear Grown-up People,

Thank you for reading our story. You do not have to read it in one go. It can be a good idea to read part of it and then stop to talk about the ideas and questions in the story.

For us children, life is like a big jigsaw puzzle. When someone we know dies, that is part of the puzzle for us too. Our way of doing the puzzle is to join the new pieces of information on to the parts we have already. It becomes difficult for us if people tell us lots of things at once. It is like being given all the pieces together and it can be confusing.

The way that seems best for us is if we can ask for the pieces of information that we need, and only be given those pieces. When we need more we can always ask. We can also get tired of doing the jigsaw puzzle of life. After even a short time we may want to go and watch TV or do something else. We hope that you will let us feel that it is all right to do that.

When children are quite small they may want to ignore death, and be busy finding the next fun thing to do. Even for us older children, we don't want to think about it all the time.

We can feel many strange feelings. It's not always easy to tell you about them. When you tell us about what you feel and that you're still trying to make sense of the jigsaw puzzle of life, and that you've not found all the pieces – that can be a help. It lets us know that we can still be safe and have fun, even when we have questions.

Sometimes we'll be fine, just knowing that you're there and you care about us. At other times we'll want to talk and tell you how we feel. You could ask us if we dream, and what we dream about, and tell us about yours.

In talking and sharing we found that we're like grown-up people, because when something bad happens we try to pretend it isn't true, or we try to blame somebody for what has happened. We've seen grown ups do this too, even when no one is to blame. Once Steve wondered if he had caused Joe to die, because of the way he pulled one of his toys away from him, when Joe was starting to chew it. Some children at our school said that death is like a punishment for something wrong. But we know that is not true, and that Steve had nothing to do with Joe's problems. We now know that Joe had a heart that was wrong, and what happened was sad, but true.

Because Mum and Dad talked to us and listened to our questions, we were able cry when we needed, or be on our own, or go out with Mudge. They also let us choose if we wanted to go to the funeral service for Joe.

If they'd not talked to us we'd probably have thought that we'd done something bad, and must be left out. We might even have wondered if what was happening was so frightening they couldn't talk – and that would have made us very frightened. When we don't get the pieces of the jigsaw that we want, when we ask, then we make them up from our imagination. Usually they're more frightening than the real answers. So telling us in words that we know, makes it clear, and that's good.

We will be thinking of you, and send our love,

Gill and Steve (and Mudge)

P.S. We're glad that life doesn't end, and that God has plans for us to live with him. Mum and Dad showed us some words from the Bible and helped us think about what they mean. The words from the Bible were:

- *Death is a bad thing, it takes our friends away.*

  "Christ must rule until God defeats all his enemies and puts them under his feet. The last enemy to be defeated is death." 1 Corinthians 15. 25–26

- *But it is safe to die. Jesus gives new life and a special home in heaven.*

  "Do not be worried and upset," Jesus told them. "Believe in God and believe also in me. There are many rooms in my Father's house, and I am going to prepare a place for you. I will come back and take you to myself so that you will be where I am." John 14. 1–3

  "God himself will be with them, and he will be their God. He will wipe away all tears from their eyes. There will be no more death, no more grief or crying or pain." Revelation 21. 3–4

- *We shall have a new body and leave the old behind.*

  "For we know that when this tent we live in – our body here on earth – is torn down, God will have a house in heaven for us to live in, a home he himself has made, which will last forever." 2 Corinthians 5. 1

- *God will be there and take away fear.*

"Even though I go through the deepest darkness, I will not be afraid, Lord, for you are with me." Psalm 23. 4

- *God shows his love for children.*

"Jesus said, 'Let the children come to me, and do not stop them, because the Kingdom of Heaven belongs to such as these.'" Mark 10. 14

"See that you don't despise any of these little ones. Their angels in heaven, I tell you, are always in the presence of my Father in heaven. Your Father in heaven does not want any of these little ones to be lost." Matthew 18. 10, 14

- *God shares our sadnesses.*

"Let us give thanks to the God and Father of our Lord Jesus Christ, the merciful Father, the God from whom all help comes! He helps us in all our troubles, so that we are able to help others who have all kinds of troubles, using the same help that we ourselves have received from God." 2 Corinthians 1. 3, 4.

(From the *Good News Bible* published by the Bible Societies and HarperCollins Publishers, © American Bible Society 1994, used with permission.)

Related titles published by National Society/Church House Publishing

Children and Bereavement

Wendy Duffy

This sensitive guide examines the needs of bereaved children of different ages, their reactions to death, and the stages of their grief. Written in non-jargon language, it provides clear, accessible information and stories of real situations.

Detailed resource lists of helpful organisations and suitable books for children, their friends, family and leaders are included.

Prayers for Children

Christopher Herbert

This is a rich and imaginative resource book which will inspire parents, teachers, clergy and everyone involved in nurturing children's faith. It is a comprehensive anthology of over five hundred prayers, suitable for church, school and home use. There are forty-five themes including *Creation, Family and Friends, Our Senses* and *Our Feelings*.

Traditional prayers stand alongside new ones; prayers of quietness next to prayers of praise. There are prayers for times of darkness and grief, and prayers for times of sunshine and joy.

The National Society

The National Society (Church of England) for Promoting Religious Education supports everyone involved in Christian education – teachers, school governors, students, parents, clergy, parish and diocesan education teams – with the resources of its RE centres, courses, conferences and archives.

Founded in 1811, the Society was chiefly responsible for setting up the nationwide network of Church schools in England and Wales, and still helps them with legal and administrative advice for headteachers and governors. It was also a pioneer in teacher education through the Church colleges. The Society now provides resources for those responsible for RE and worship in any school, lecturers and students in colleges, and clergy and lay people in parish education. It publishes a wide range of books and booklets and the magazine *Together with Children* for leaders of children's work.

The National Society is a voluntary body that works in partnership with the Church of England General Synod Board of Education and the Division for Education of the Church of Wales. An Anglican society, it also operates ecumenically, and helps to promote inter-faith education and dialogue through its RE centres.

For a free resources catalogue and details of individual, corporate and associate membership contact:

> The Promotions Officer
> The National Society
> Church House
> Great Smith Street
> London SW1P 3NZ
> Telephone: 0171-222 1672
> Fax: 0171-233 2592